D0759766

MICROSCOPIC
Scary Creatures

Written by
Ian Graham

Created and designed
by David Salariya

Franklin Watts®
An Imprint of Scholastic Inc.
NEW YORK • TORONTO • LONDON • AUCKLAND • SYDNEY
MEXICO CITY • NEW DELHI • HONG KONG
DANBURY, CONNECTICUT

Author:

Ian Graham studied applied physics
at the City University, London. He then earned a
postgraduate degree in journalism, specializing in
science and technology. Since becoming a freelance
author and journalist, he has written more than
one hundred children's nonfiction books.

Artists:

Carolyn Scrace
Janet Baker and Julian Baker
  (JB Illustrations)
John Francis

Series Creator:

David Salariya was born in Dundee,
Scotland. In 1989 he established The Salariya Book
Company. He has illustrated a wide range of books
and has created many new series for publishers in the
UK and overseas. He lives in Brighton, England, with
his wife, illustrator Shirley Willis, and their son.

Editor: Jamie Pitman

Editorial Assistant:
Rob Walker

Picture Research:
Mark Bergin, Carolyn Franklin

Photo Credits:

t=top, b=bottom

fotolia: 5t, 6, 10, 12, 18, 22, 23, 26
iStockphoto: 5b, 7, 21, 24, 27, 29

PAPER FROM
SUSTAINABLE
FORESTS

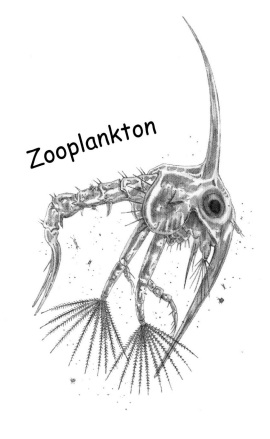

Zooplankton

© The Salariya Book Company Ltd MMIX

Created, designed, and produced by
The Salariya Book Company Ltd
25 Marlborough Place, Brighton BN1 1UB

A CIP catalog record for this title is available
from the Library of Congress.

ISBN-13: 978-0-531-21673-6 (lib. bdg.)
978-0-531-21044-4 (pbk.)
ISBN-10: 0-531-21673-X (lib. bdg.)
0-531-21044-8 (pbk.)

Published in 2010 in the United States by
Franklin Watts
An Imprint of Scholastic Inc.
557 Broadway
New York, NY 10012

Printed in China

Contents

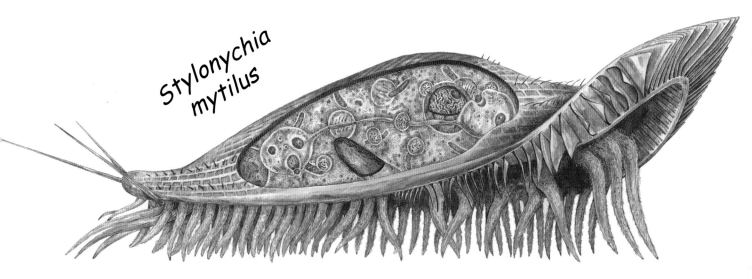

Stylonychia mytilus

What Are Microscopic Creatures?

Cilia

Food particles move this way

Microscopic creatures are animals and animal-like creatures that are extremely small. Some of them are so small that they can be seen only with a powerful **microscope**.

Others are just big enough to be seen with the naked eye, but you would need a microscope to see them clearly.

Although these creatures are tiny, some of them look like monsters from another world. The tiniest of these are called **protozoa**. A protozoan is made of just one living **cell**.

Stentor polymorphus (cutaway view)

Stentor polymorphus is a trumpet-shaped protozoan (single-celled animal) that lives in **freshwater**. It is just .05 inches (1.2 mm) long. It is covered with short hairs called **cilia**. The cilia around the trumpet's rim beat back and forth to sweep food particles into its body.

Deer tick
.08 inches (2 mm) long

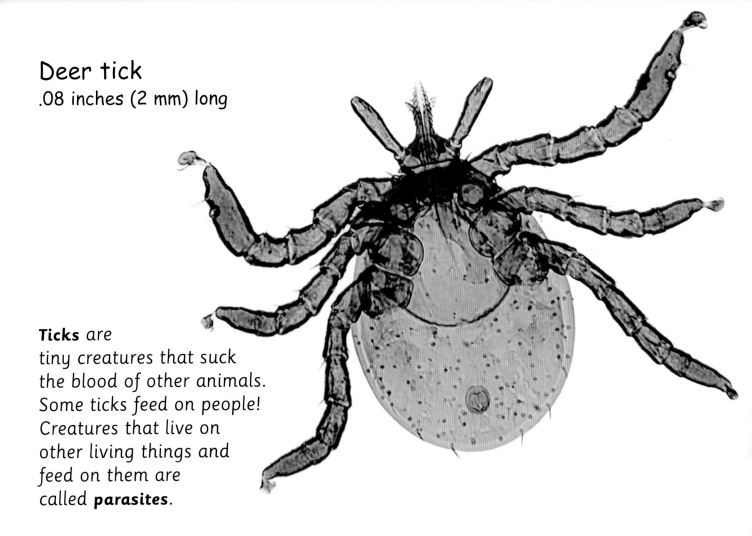

Ticks are tiny creatures that suck the blood of other animals. Some ticks feed on people! Creatures that live on other living things and feed on them are called **parasites**.

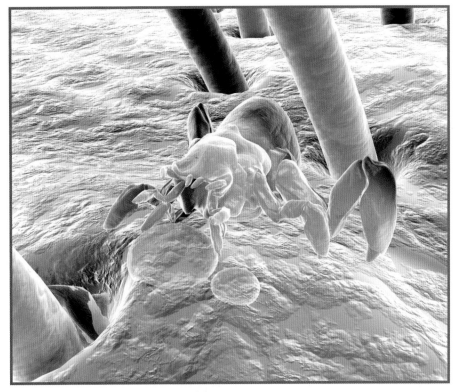

Mite seen through an electron microscope

Mites are tiny crawling creatures that are usually less than .04 inches (1 mm) long. Many of them are a lot smaller. They look like little dark dots, if you can see them at all.

Mites and ticks have their skeletons on the outside of their bodies. These external skeletons are called **exoskeletons**. They protect the soft inside parts of creatures' bodies.

Where Do Microscopic Creatures Live?

Microscopic creatures are found nearly everywhere. They live in rivers, the sea, and soil, and on garden plants and in forests. They live in soggy marshes and dust-dry deserts. They're found on top of mountains and at the icy poles. They even live in your home and on your body, but they're so small that you usually don't notice them.

Dust mites live in bedding, old clothing, and couches.

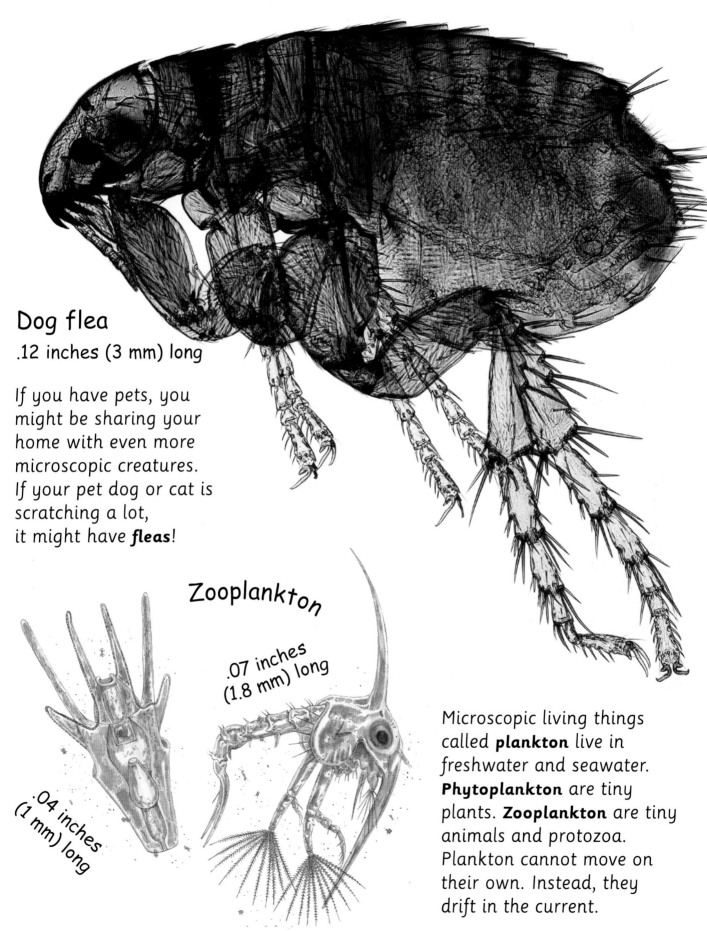

Dog flea

.12 inches (3 mm) long

If you have pets, you
might be sharing your
home with even more
microscopic creatures.
If your pet dog or cat is
scratching a lot,
it might have **fleas**!

Zooplankton

.07 inches
(1.8 mm) long

.04 inches
(1 mm) long

Microscopic living things
called **plankton** live in
freshwater and seawater.
Phytoplankton are tiny
plants. **Zooplankton** are tiny
animals and protozoa.
Plankton cannot move on
their own. Instead, they
drift in the current.

How Do Such Tiny Creatures Get Around?

Many microscopic creatures move about to hunt for food and escape from danger. Some of them get around by walking.

Fleas are great jumpers. They can leap high into the air to hop onto an animal or to escape a **predator**.

Some microscopic creatures that live in water can swim, but others just drift in the current. They wait for food to come to them.

Rotifers are tiny creatures that live in water. They are .002 inches (.04 mm) to .08 inches (2 mm) long and made of about 1,000 cells. Their mouths are surrounded by cilia that sweep food into their bodies. Some rotifers swim around. Others stay in one place, stuck to a rock.

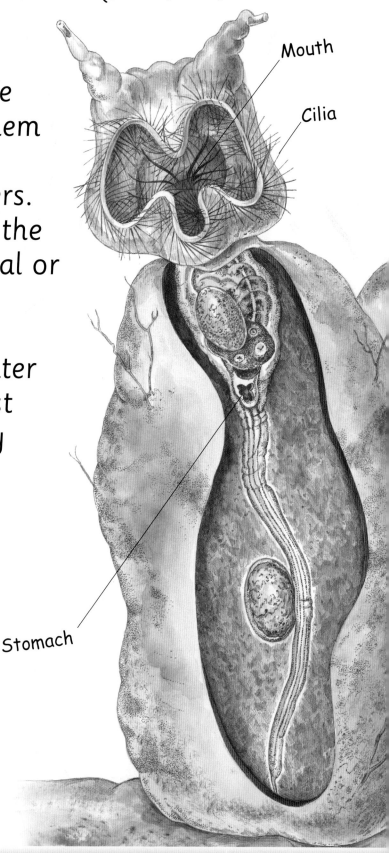

Rotifer
(cutaway view)

Mouth

Cilia

Stomach

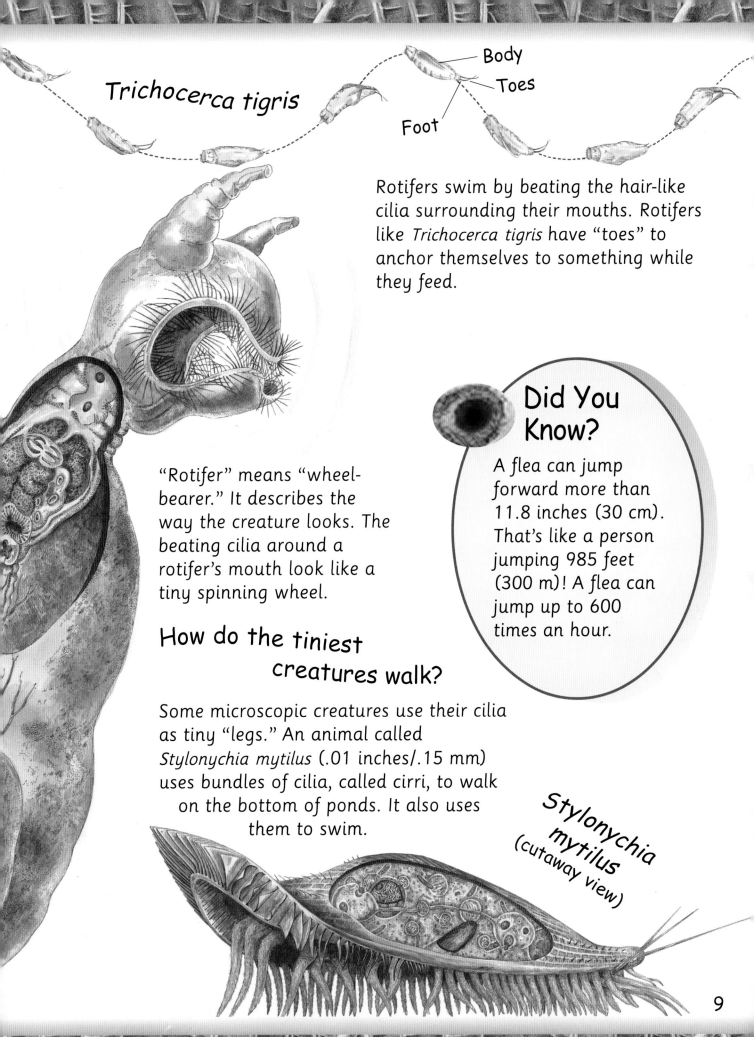

Trichocerca tigris

Body

Toes

Foot

Rotifers swim by beating the hair-like cilia surrounding their mouths. Rotifers like *Trichocerca tigris* have "toes" to anchor themselves to something while they feed.

"Rotifer" means "wheel-bearer." It describes the way the creature looks. The beating cilia around a rotifer's mouth look like a tiny spinning wheel.

How do the tiniest creatures walk?

Some microscopic creatures use their cilia as tiny "legs." An animal called *Stylonychia mytilus* (.01 inches/.15 mm) uses bundles of cilia, called cirri, to walk on the bottom of ponds. It also uses them to swim.

Did You Know?

A flea can jump forward more than 11.8 inches (30 cm). That's like a person jumping 985 feet (300 m)! A flea can jump up to 600 times an hour.

Stylonychia mytilus
(cutaway view)

9

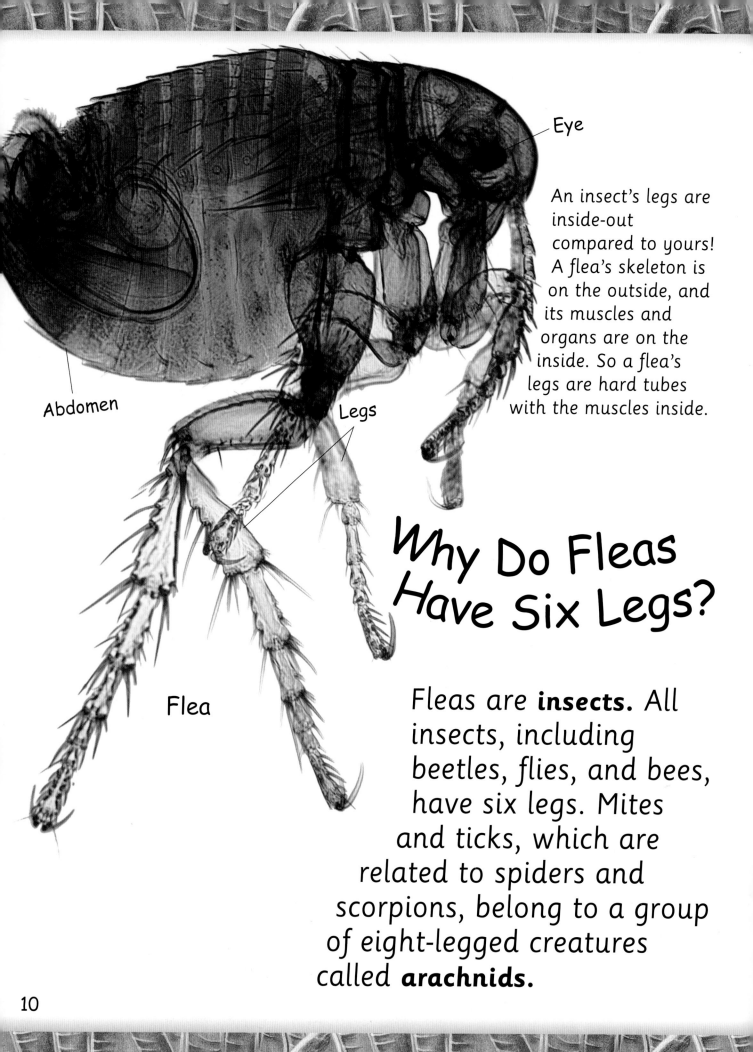

Eye

An insect's legs are inside-out compared to yours! A flea's skeleton is on the outside, and its muscles and organs are on the inside. So a flea's legs are hard tubes with the muscles inside.

Abdomen

Legs

Why Do Fleas Have Six Legs?

Flea

Fleas are **insects.** All insects, including beetles, flies, and bees, have six legs. Mites and ticks, which are related to spiders and scorpions, belong to a group of eight-legged creatures called **arachnids.**

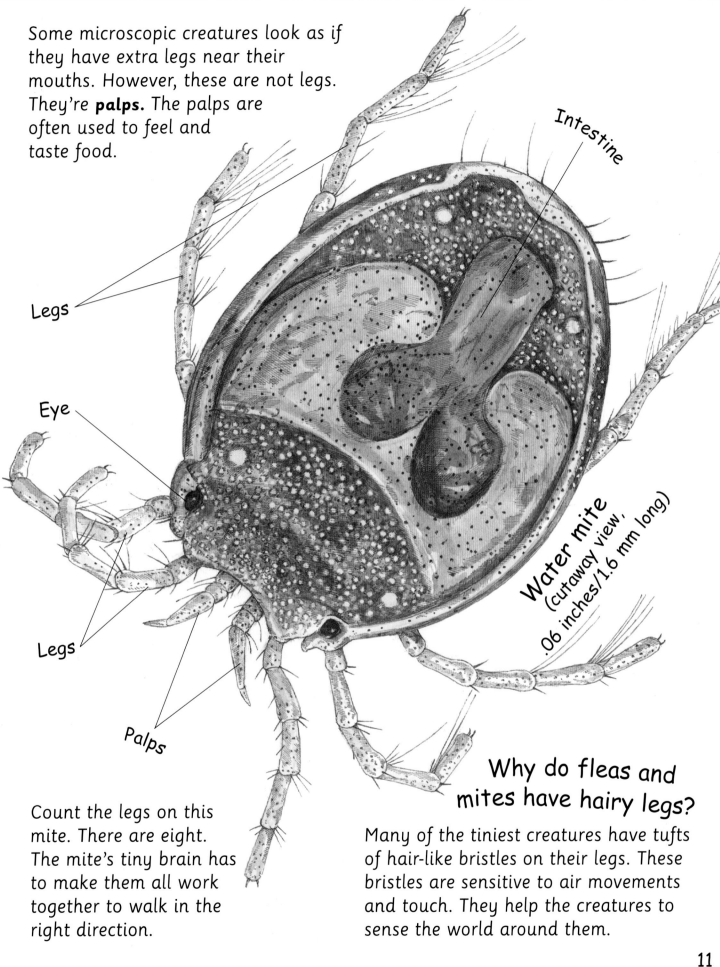

Some microscopic creatures look as if they have extra legs near their mouths. However, these are not legs. They're **palps.** The palps are often used to feel and taste food.

Legs

Eye

Legs

Palps

Intestine

Water mite
(cutaway view,
.06 inches/1.6 mm long)

Count the legs on this mite. There are eight. The mite's tiny brain has to make them all work together to walk in the right direction.

Why do fleas and mites have hairy legs?

Many of the tiniest creatures have tufts of hair-like bristles on their legs. These bristles are sensitive to air movements and touch. They help the creatures to sense the world around them.

Dust mite

What Do Microscopic Creatures Eat?

Tiny creatures eat tiny things. Dust mites eat the flakes of skin that they find in the pillows, couches, and other objects in your home. Lots of microscopic creatures feed on plants. Some have sharp jaws for munching through leaves, while others have needle-like mouth parts for making holes in plants to suck out sap.

What are predators?

Predators are creatures that hunt and kill other animals for food. Some microscopic creatures are predators. *Actinosphaerium eichhornii* is a predator. It's just one big ball-shaped cell, .03 inches (.8 mm) across, with lots of spiny "arms" sticking out. It drifts around freshwater ponds and lakes, capturing bits of food with its arms and digesting them.

Actinosphaerium eichhornii
(cutaway view)

How do bloodsuckers feed?

Fleas and ticks have mouth parts that are strong and sharp enough to cut through an animal's skin. Then they suck out blood.

Did You Know?

In just one day, a cat flea can suck as much as 15 times its own body weight in blood out of a cat.

How Long Do They Live?

Small creatures usually have shorter lives than large creatures, and the smallest creatures don't live long at all. Most microscopic creatures live for just a few weeks or months.

Head lice are tiny parasites that live on human hair and skin. They live for only about a month, but they can lay up to 300 eggs in this short time. Most fleas and dust mites live for only three months or so. Ticks, however, can live from several months to two years.

What are water bears?

Water bears are tiny creatures, .05 inches (1.2 mm) long, that live in freshwater. If their bodies dry up, they can survive for many years and become active again when water returns.

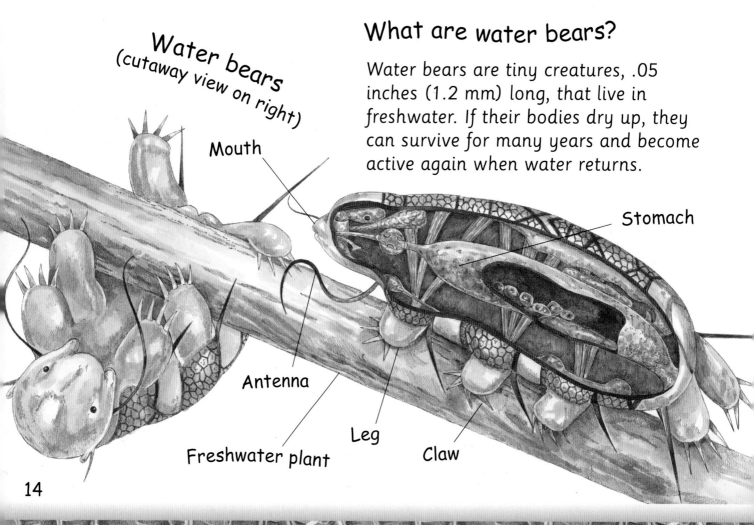

Water bears
(cutaway view on right)

Mouth

Stomach

Antenna

Leg

Claw

Freshwater plant

Did You Know?

When dried-up water bears were sent into outer space aboard a satellite, they returned unharmed, making them the first animals to survive in the **vacuum** of space.

How long does a water flea live?

The length of a water flea's life depends on the temperature of the water it lives in. At 68°F (20°C), it lives for 7 to 8 weeks. In colder water, its heart beats more slowly, and it lives longer.

How do cat fleas find cats?

An adult cat flea emerges from a **cocoon**. It can delay coming out of its cocoon for several months until a cat walks by. When the flea feels the warmth of a nearby cat or feels the vibration of its footsteps, it quickly comes out of the cocoon, leaps onto the cat, and starts sucking its blood.

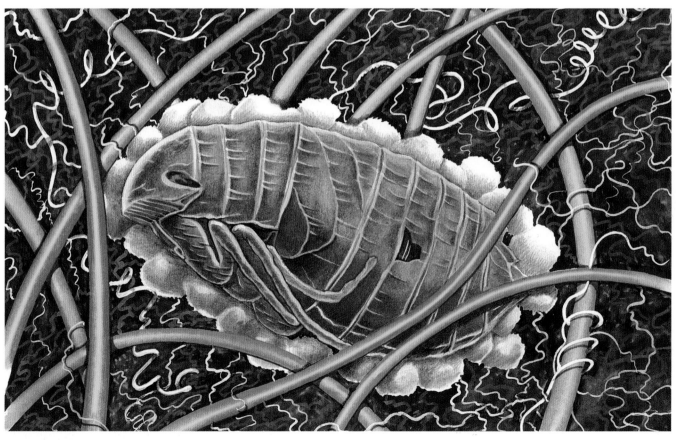

Cat flea in silk cocoon

Do These Small Creatures Bite People?

The animal a parasite lives on is called its **host**. Specific kinds of parasites live on specific kinds of hosts. For example, there are some kinds of fleas, lice, and mites that live only on people. Many of these parasites are biters. They bite you to eat your skin or drink your blood!

Cat fleas and dog fleas may bite people too, but they cannot produce eggs unless they bite cats, dogs, or certain other animals. They have to feed on the right kind of blood.

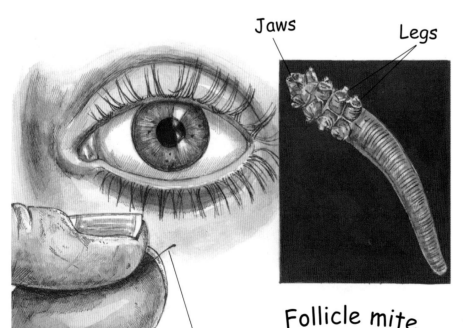

Jaws

Legs

Eyelash

Follicle mite

Thin follicle mites live inside hair follicles—the holes in the skin from which hairs grow. Follicle mites feed on skin cells and on oils that the follicle produces, so they don't have to bite. They live mainly on a person's face and head, especially in the eyelash follicles.

Mountain beaver

Beaver fur

Mountain beaver flea (enlarged)

Actual size

Did You Know?

There are more than 2,000 **species** of fleas. Cat fleas are found on both dogs and cats in North America. Dog fleas are more common in Europe.

Most fleas are .08 to .12 inches (2 to 3 mm) long and their bites are bad enough. But the flea bites a mountain beaver suffers can be even worse.

Mountain beavers live on the west coast of North America. They are host to the world's biggest flea. It's called *Hystrichopsylla schefferi*, and it's almost half an inch (12 mm) long. That's four to six times the size of other fleas!

Why Do Such Tiny Bites Itch So Much?

The bites of fleas and ticks are no bigger than pinpricks, but they can get very red, swollen, and sore. It's not the bite itself that causes the itching and pain. It's the creature's saliva, or spit, that causes trouble. Scabies mites are microscopic creatures that burrow into human skin. They eat the skin as they dig through it, and their saliva causes terrible itching.

X-Ray Vision

Hold the next page up to the light and see what's under the skin.

See what's inside

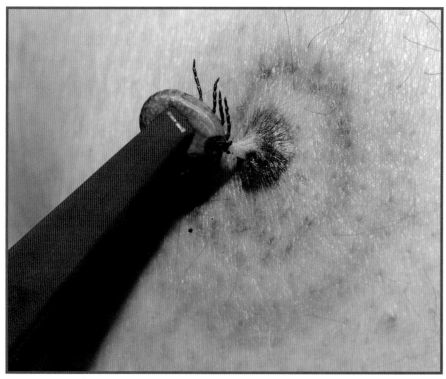

A tick being removed from human skin

Ticks are blood-sucking creatures that usually feed on pets and wild animals. However, they will bite humans too. A bite from a tick usually causes mild itching, but some people can suffer a much more painful reaction. Some ticks can spread dangerous diseases, such as Lyme disease and Rocky Mountain spotted fever.

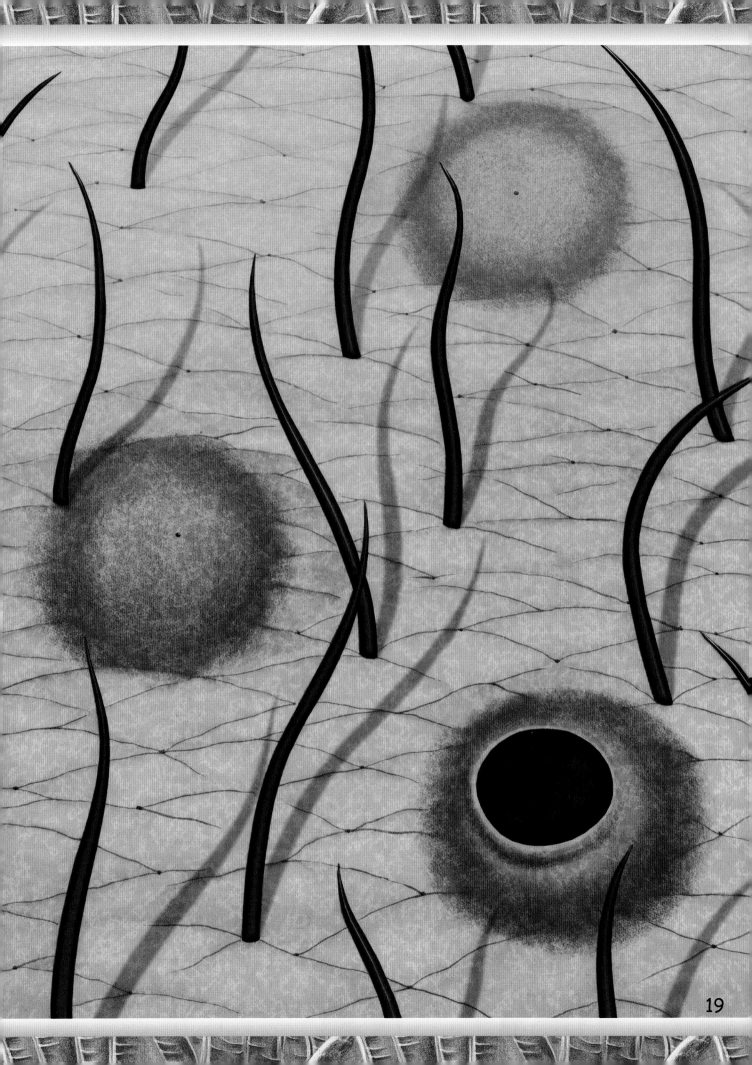

Eggs

Burrows

Scabies mite

Scabies mite

Are Microscopic Creatures Dangerous?

Some microscopic creatures are dangerous to humans and other animals because they cause diseases. A serious disease called malaria is caused by tiny protozoa spread by mosquito bites.

Parasites spread by tsetse flies cause sleeping sickness, a disease that kills 40,000 people each year.

Did You Know?

Every year, up to 500 million people are infected with diseases spread by mosquito bites. Almost three million of them die.

Mosquito piercing human skin and drinking blood

How Do Biters Find Their Victims?

Most microscopic creatures can't see, but they have other ways of finding food. They sense their victim's body heat, its breath, or the vibrations it causes when it moves.

Some microscopic creatures drift in water, infecting hosts that drink it. Others are carried to their victims by infected flies or mosquitoes.

Young wood ticks cling to bushes, but quickly fasten themselves to passing dogs, horses, or people.

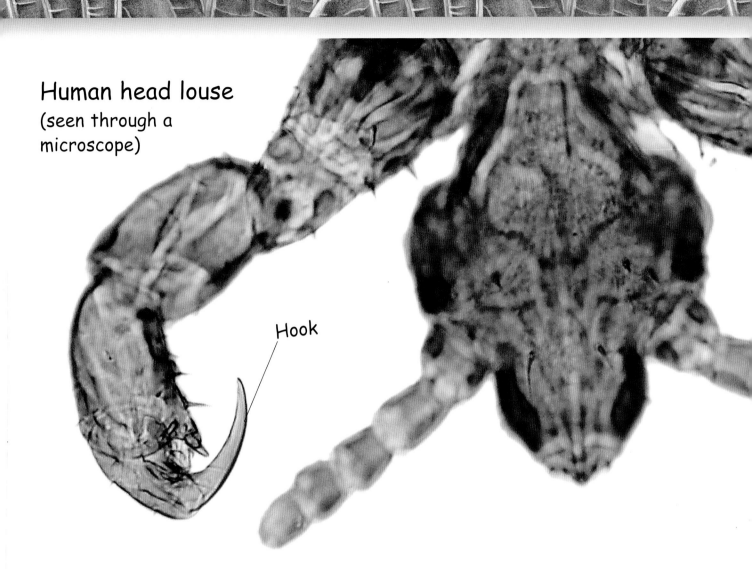

Human head louse
(seen through a
microscope)

Hook

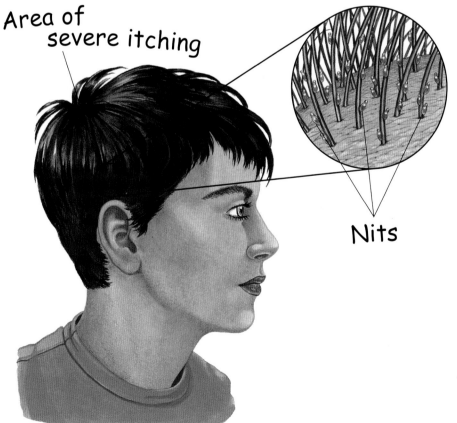

Area of
severe itching

Nits

How do
they hold on?

Creatures have developed
special ways to hold on to
their host when it moves
or scratches to get rid of
them. Head lice have
hooked legs that grip hair
tightly. They stick their
eggs to strands of the
host's hair to stop them
from falling off. The eggs
are called nits.

What Do Microscopic Creatures Do to Plants?

Microscopic creatures may be tiny, but they can damage and even destroy plants.
Insects called thrips, less than a millimeter long, make holes in plants and suck out the sap. Holes made by thrips and other creatures also let in **viruses**, **bacteria**, and *fungi*, which cause even more damage to the plant.

X-Ray Vision

Hold the next page up to the light and see what's eating the wheat.

See what's inside

Spider mites are tiny arachnids that feed on plant sap. Thousands of mites can suck out so much sap that a plant's leaves turn yellow and die. Without enough leaves to make food, the plant may die as well.

Red spider mite from Kenya, Africa

Ear of wheat

Thrips

What Are Larvae?

When the egg of a tiny insect such as a flea hatches, the wormlike creature that comes out is called a **larva**.

The larva grows for a while and then seals itself inside a case, or cocoon. Inside, it becomes a **pupa**, which then changes into the adult insect. Some sea creatures, such as shrimps, crabs, and lobsters, start their lives as microscopic larvae too.

Did You Know?

When a cat flea larva spins a cocoon around itself, bits of fluff stick to the cocoon and make it look like a harmless bit of carpet fluff.

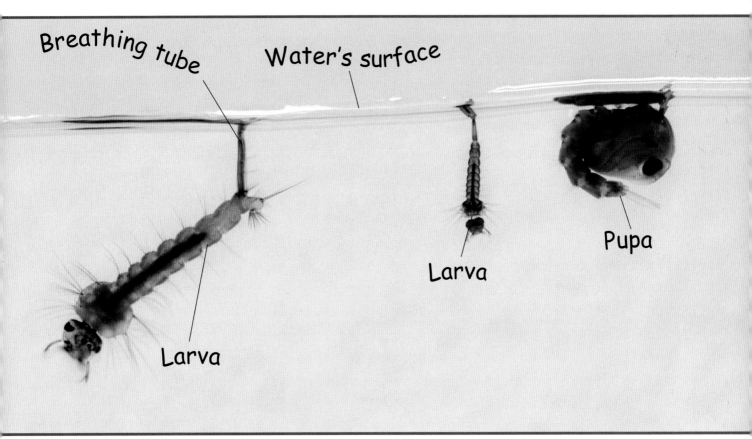

Breathing tube

Water's surface

Larva

Pupa

Larva

Mosquito larvae and pupa

Can Microscopic Creatures Be Good for Us?

Not all microscopic creatures harm plants or spread diseases. Some of them can be helpful. One way to deal with the **pests** that damage plants is to attack them with creatures such as tiny flies and wasps. Using creatures instead of chemicals to kill pests is called biological control.

How can wasps help us?

A tiny wasp called *Encarsia formosa* is used to control the whitefly, an insect that infests plants in greenhouses. The wasps lay their eggs inside the whitefly. When the eggs hatch, the grubs eat the whitefly alive!

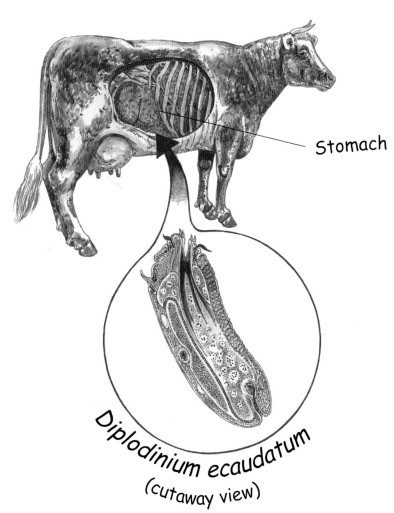

Stomach

Diplodinium ecaudatum
(cutaway view)

How do microscopic creatures help cows?

Cows eat a lot of grass, which contains a substance called **cellulose**. Cows can't digest cellulose on their own, but the bacteria and protozoa living in their stomach can. One of the protozoa that do this vital job is called *Diplodinium ecaudatum*.

Did You Know?

Garden slugs can be controlled by tiny wormlike creatures called nematodes. The nematodes multiply inside the slugs and kill them from within.

Wasps can be used to control the tomato hornworm, a pest that destroys tomato plants. This hornworm is covered with wasp cocoons. Wasp larvae hatched inside the caterpillar and then ate their way out.

Microscopic Facts

Mites are among the oldest known creatures. There are fossils of mites that are 400 million years old. There are more than 45,000 known species of mites, and scientists think there are a lot more still to be discovered.

During their pupal stage, insects can't move. They can't run from predators, so larvae hide before they change into pupae. Pupae are often colored to match their surroundings, or disguised so they're hard to spot.

A flea's body is long and thin. This makes it easy for the flea to squeeze through an animal's fur, hair, or feathers.

If a flea were to lay eggs and the resulting fleas kept breeding, there would be 10,000 fleas in just one month!

On each of a tick's first two legs is a part called Haller's organ. It senses heat and carbon dioxide. Ticks feed on warm-blooded animals, which breathe out carbon dioxide. Haller's organ helps ticks to find their victims by tracking the carbon dioxide.

Ticks can spread a variety of diseases to people, pets, and wild animals. One of these is called Lyme disease. It causes headaches, swelling, and joint and muscle pain. In some cases, it can be a very serious illness.

When your skin is cut and bleeds, the bleeding soon stops. The blood thickens and forms a clot that plugs the cut. This is called coagulation. When a flea or tick bites through skin, it injects a substance called an anti-coagulant. It stops the blood from forming a clot, so the blood keeps flowing and the flea or tick can keep feeding.

Zooplankton

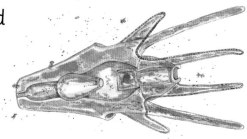

Glossary

arachnid An eight-legged animal. There are more than 50,000 different species of arachnid.

bacteria Single-celled microorganisms, some of which carry diseases.

cell The smallest unit, or building block, of a plant or animal. Protozoa and bacteria are made up of just one cell.

cellulose The substance that makes up most of the cell walls in a plant.

cilia Tiny hair-like parts of a cell. Some cilia beat back and forth to guide food into a creature's mouth; others may help it to swim.

cocoon A protective case that houses an insect during its pupal stage.

exoskeleton A skeleton that covers the outside of a creature.

flea A wingless, blood-sucking insect; fleas are parasites that feed on warm-blooded animals.

freshwater Water from lakes and rivers which, unlike seawater, is not salty.

fungi Microorganisms that can grow to become visible to the eye, for example in the form of mushrooms and toadstools.

host The animal or plant that a parasite lives on.

insect A small animal with six legs and an exoskeleton.

larva (plural **larvae**) A wormlike creature that hatches from an insect egg. The larva later changes into an adult creature.

microscope A scientific tool that uses lenses to produce enlarged images of small objects.

microscopic So small that it can be seen only through a microscope.

mite A tiny eight-legged creature related to spiders.

palps Feelers for touch or taste near the head of an insect or other small creature.

parasite A creature that lives on a larger creature and feeds on it.

pest A creature that harms humans or their crops.

plankton Small plants (**phytoplankton**) and animals and protozoa (**zooplankton**) that drift with water currents in seas, rivers, lakes, and ponds.

predator A creature that kills and eats other creatures.

protozoan (plural **protozoa**) An animal-like creature consisting of only one cell.

pupa The stage of an insect's life when it changes from a larva into an adult insect.

rotifer A tiny creature that lives in water and has cilia around its mouth that look like spinning wheels.

species A group of animals or plants that look alike and can breed with each other.

tick A small, blood-sucking creature related to spiders.

vacuum Space that is empty of air and anything else.

virus A microbe that needs to enter a living cell to grow. Viruses cause a large number of diseases in plants, animals, and humans.

Index